Wolfgang Rug · Thomas Neumann
Andreas Tomaszewski

50 PRACTICAL TIPS
FOR LEARNING GERMAN

Translated by Edna McCown

Klett Edition Deutsch

1. Auflage   1   5   4   3   2 | 1997   96   95

© Verlag Klett Edition Deutsch GmbH, München 1993
Zeichnungen: Sepp Buchegger, Tübingen
Druck: Paul Schäuble OHG, Stuttgart
Alle Rechte vorbehalten · Printed in Germany

ISBN 3-12-**675384**-1

TABLE OF CONTENTS

GERMAN WITH GERMANS
 1 Language Tandem
 2 Don't Panic!
 3 Help Questions
 4 Could You Help Me?
 5 The Courage to Make Small-talk
 6 Missed Opportunities
 7 Training for the Competent
 8 German in the Ear
 9 An Invitation to Germans
10 Get Out of Your Room!
11 Show Your Own Culture

WORDS
12 Word-scraps
13 Excursions into a Dictionary
14 Don't Touch that Dictionary!
15 Word-groups
16 Stick-on Memos
17 "Snapped-up" Idioms
18 "Foreign" Words are Not so Foreign
19 My Terminology Dictionary

GRAMMAR
20 Practicing Nonsense
21 House Altar
22 My Favorite Mistakes
23 Mistake Immunization
24 Recording Your Mistakes
25 Correct Me – I'll Show You How
26 German Diagnosis
27 My Grammar on Cards
28 Sentence Decoding
29 Phrase Practice
30 Define What You Want to Learn
31 Working with Workbooks

TEXTS
32 Learn by Memorizing
33 Rapid-reading
34 Reading with a Marker
35 Collectibles

36 My favorite Texts
37 Bedside Reading
38 Learning with Comics
39 Taking More Professional Notes
40 More Professional Texts
41 Reading Aloud, Declamation

GERMAN IN GERMANY
42 "Conquer" Germany
43 Diary of Foreignness
44 My German Diary
45 Separating from Your Compatriots
46 My Second Work Space
47 My Daily Newspaper
48 Books Useful in Learning German
49 Masked Foreigners
50 Creative Reflection on Learning German

ABOVE ALL...

Each of the following **50 Tips for Learning German** begins with "The Way It Is." Learning a new language is a process which requires a great deal of time and effort, especially when it is the German language, with its complex rules of grammar and many endings, its particular sentence structure and many complicated words, the jungle of its dialects and the monotony of many textbooks. All of these contribute little to the fun of learning. We offer **50 Tips** to demonstrate that learning German can be fun, can be amusing and stimulating, and that even the difficult stages can have their pleasures. These **50 Tips** will challenge your creativity and utilize your enjoyment of play and experimentation.

We are saying that one learns only what one finds enjoyable, and also that to learn is to have new experiences.

For this reason, learning German is not an isolated activity to be carried out behind closed doors. (Though it is true that a certain amount of this is necessary.) Above all, learning German is learning about a country, its people, and its culture, its everyday life and unique features. We are not saying that you should learn German *in order to* get to know Germany and the Germans. Rather, you will learn German **through** getting to know Germany and the Germans. And we can tell you in advance that you will come to know yourself and your own culture better in the process.

These **50 Tips** show you *how* to do this. They are 50 practical proposals, ideas, and methods to help you set off on your path with increased self-confidence.

This path usually begins in your native country. Several of the **50 Tips** apply only to Germany. But with a little imagination, you can adapt them for use in your own country.

Once you have learned how to learn, you will continue to do so, even when there is no language class or textbook, no teacher to ask for help. You will have become independent and able find your way alone. These **50 Tips** will accompany you until you no longer need them.

Tübingen, Fall 1991
Wolfgang Rug
Thomas Neumann
Andreas Tomaszewski

1 GERMAN WITH GERMANS
LANGUAGE TANDEM

THE WAY IT IS (POSSIBLY):

He, she, they, you: Whoever comes to Germany becomes a foreigner at the border, which is not always a great feeling. You don't know your way around, you're afraid of making mistakes and you do make mistakes, you feel dumb, or are treated as if you are. You aren't yourself, you may experience a crisis of identity, culturally and personally.

But Germans are foreigners as well ("your" foreigners), and there are those among them who wish to learn your language, get to know your country, your culture, and you. And you are an appropriate partner and teacher for them.

WHAT TO DO?

Find a tandem partner, your tandem partner (a tandem is a bicycle for two). As part of a team, each of you is teacher and student for the other. Don't be shy, jump right in!

HOW?

Perhaps there is someone who could facilitate a tandem partnership where you live, work, or study.

Post a notice with your address and telephone number on the bulletin board of your dormitory or German language institute, or institute where your native language is taught. There are many possibilities.

Make it known that you are a language partner in search of a partner for yourself.

WE RECOMMEND:

Talk with your partner about things you and s/he are interested in.
Come to a precise agreement on the activities you will share.
It is absolutely important that you agree to speak German 50% of the time and your language 50% of the time.
Agree on a set time (once a week for two hours, for example), and leave time open for a further meeting if you have the time and inclination.

CONCRETELY:

You may wish to do the following (and much more): Talk about yourself and your country; tell a story; talk spontaneously; help each other learn; read texts together or work on your own texts; correct mistakes; go places together; discuss movies and TV programs; cook a meal together; drink tea...(think up your own activities).

2 GERMAN WITH GERMANS
DON'T PANIC!

THE WAY IT IS (FOR MANY):
When learning a foreign language, particularly as an adult, you may feel any of the following: I don't understand anything at all; I feel totally lost; I don't get it; I'm not making any progress; I'll never be able to understand German. These feelings can result in frustration, confusion, or panic. (This may be the case, above all, if German is the first foreign language you have ever learned.)

WHAT TO DO?
Talk openly about how you feel, make your feelings public—to your friends, others in your language class, the Germans you communicate with, your teacher. Don't be afraid to appear stupid or confused: You may be sure that others feel the same way. And they will feel better if they see that you, too, are experiencing the same situation as they. Make of your difficulties a subject that others can relate to.

HOW?
Quite simply: Talk about what is bothering you, and how you feel about it. Have the courage to reveal your situation. The main problem, after all, is that often you don't trust yourself to talk about it.

Don't be afraid of disturbing your partners. (They should listen to what you have to say.)

Don't be afraid to disturb your teacher. (S/he's being paid for such things.)

Don't be afraid to interrupt the lesson. (You will be making instruction more human, more interesting and productive.)

CONCRETELY:
Ask the classmate sitting next to you questions if you don't know something (and s/he will then ask you in turn.)

Ask questions during instruction.

Ask your teacher to hold "office hours."

At the end of the instruction hour or day, ask yourself if you were able to do the above. If not, try again tomorrow.

AND FURTHERMORE:
There are always difficulties involved in learning a new language. It is hard work and requires much effort, and this is something you will have to accept. But your feelings are a part of you and of your progress. If you are able to accept your partial ignorance, then you are learning at an adult level. You are an adult member of an intercultural learning group, and that is a meaningful and interesting role to play (see tips 1 and 43).

3 GERMAN WITH GERMANS
HELP QUESTIONS

THE WAY IT IS (IN MANY SITUATIONS):

When learning a foreign language, you may often feel isolated, alone, without help: What does this word mean?; I understood none of what was just said; What did that person just say? Often you will not possess the linguistic or communicative skills to resolve certain situations (see tips 2.5 and 4).

WHAT TO DO?

You need a small number of useful questions you can call upon automatically.

HOW?

First, clarify which recurring situations are causing feelings of helplessness; formulate simple, clear, easily asked questions or requests to deal with these situations.

CONCRETELY:

Here are 10 examples:
  1. Was bedeutet dieses Wort?
  2. Würden Sie mir bitte den letzten Satz noch einmal wiederholen.
  3. Entschuldigung, ich habe das nicht ganz verstanden.
  4. Was hat sie gerade gesagt? Was haben Sie gerade gesagt?
  5. Du, lies mir das bitte einmal vor!
  6. Kannst du mir kurz erklären, was in dem Text steht?
  7. Weißt du, wie das Wort... geschrieben wird?
  8. Ist das richtig, was ich hier geschrieben habe?
  9. Was war denn falsch?
  10. Hast du mich verstanden?

WE RECOMMEND:

Write these (or similar) questions in block letters on pieces of paper and post them at home, until you are totally familiar with them. Write them down on a piece of paper that you keep at your desk in language class.
Make a note of how often you use this method, and in which situations you should have used it.

AND FURTHERMORE:

You may also employ this method when it is not truly necessary, simply in order to practice it, or to communicate with your neighbor.

4 GERMAN WITH GERMANS
COULD YOU HELP ME?

THE WAY IT IS (MUCH TOO OFTEN):
The German class is a sheltered place; there is a teacher who is paid to help you learn; and there are other foreigners who have the same problems as you, and who sometimes may be able to help and sometimes not. But when class is over, most students are on their own: doing homework, reading texts and the newspaper, studying for tests, going over specialized material. There are Germans nearby who could help, but no contact with them has been established.

WHAT TO DO?
Ask Germans sitting, standing, or living nearby for a little help. You will see that you will often receive it, and establish friendly and helpful contacts in the process. Be prepared to occasionally experience rejection or frustration. But your experience fundamentally will be positive.

HOW?
As we have already said: You must know how to ask a question (see tip 3). So ask: State clearly what it is you want to know and roughly how long it will take. The rest will follow.

CONCRETELY:
You are confronted daily with the appropriate opportunities: in the cafeteria or restaurant, in a cafe, or on the train, or waiting somewhere on a bench, or in the hallway of your building: *Darf ich Sie etwas fragen? Ich habe hier für meinen Deutschkurs Hausaufgaben gemacht; können Sie die Sätze bitte einmal lesen und mir sagen, ob etwas falsch ist?... Du, ich brauche eine deutsche Stimme für eine Aufnahme, kannst du mir ein paar Texte auf Kassette sprechen? Es wird etwa eine halbe Stunde dauern.* In a bookstore: *Können Sie mir helfen? Ich suche/Wo finde ich...* Other possibilities will present themselves: You might need help editing a text you have written, or help with a poem in German, or in preparing a report for a seminar (which certainly will take longer), or help with filling out a form or understanding operation instructions...

WE RECOMMEND:
That you not hesitate in requesting such help. There is no cause to have a bad conscience. Leave it to the other person to say no if s/he doesn't choose to help, or truly does not have the time. Don't exaggerate your gratitude at their response. Don't be disappointed if someone refuses to help you.

AND FURTHERMORE:
No one will hinder you in inviting your new helper to have a cup of coffee at a cafe. But it is not necessary to do so.

5 GERMAN WITH GERMANS
THE COURAGE TO MAKE SMALL-TALK

THE WAY IT IS (ALMOST DAILY):

As a foreigner, you might feel timid and shy when you are with Germans. But shyness will not help you to learn German. If you do not trust yourself to open your mouth and speak to them, Germans easily may appear inaccessible or not very friendly. If you do not make contact with them, you have little opportunity to converse with them, and your time is being wasted.

WHAT TO DO?

It would be helpful to have at your disposal a few German sentences which deal with everyday situations, and which will allow you to make small talk. This, of course, is also a question of temperament. Nor is one always in the mood to talk with others. But if you are in the mood, you should know how to initiate a conversation.

It is not necessary always to be reserved or overly polite. Be as bold as you wish.

WE RECOMMEND:

Prepare a few conversation-openers (10 sentences, for example) to fit everyday situations that often recur, and that you are familiar with.

CONCRETELY:

What do you say when you wish to join someone's table at a restaurant? (*Ist der Platz noch frei?* is preferable to *Darf ich mich zu Ihnen setzen?*)

What do you say to a salesperson, for example, when you are trying on a sweater and wish to see a larger selection?

What words do you use when you wish to engage fellow train passengers in conversation? (You might suggest going to the dining car for a cup of coffee, for example.)

How do you invite your neighbor to tea?

Which expressions can be used in asking for a small favor, for example, in reading a map or carrying a bag, for assistance in a bookstore, or in filling out a form, or for directions at the university, and how does one initiate small-talk?

Ask for the recipe when you enjoy the way something tastes, and the contact is made.

AND FURTHERMORE:

Once again: Don't be too polite or reserved. Politeness often masks your own fear and, pardon us for saying so, a certain cowardice. Germans are not as distant as they seem, or have the reputation for being. Many Germans will welcome the encounter.

Also: If an experience doesn't go particularly well, it is easy to break off the conversation by simply walking away (with an appropriate comment). No great damage is done.

6 GERMAN WITH GERMANS
MISSED OPPORTUNITIES

THE WAY IT IS (TOO OFTEN, UNFORTUNATELY):
There are many people who wish to learn German, but who often miss the opportunity to speak German. Many language course students are afraid to talk, and sit for hours in silence. Many can't seem to open their mouths in the company of Germans. This, however, is disheartening, boring, and unproductive.

WHAT TO DO?
Try to take advantage of your opportunities. Use your time wisely.

HOW?
We have already listed several methods showing how to make conversation and come in contact with Germans (see tips 3, 4, and 5). We suggest that every evening you evaluate how much German you have spoken that day, what hindered you in speaking more, what you are afraid of, and what you would change. The next day, try a little harder.

WE RECOMMEND:
Speak to your teacher about the fact that you are speaking too little German, and together figure out how you can participate more.
Ask more questions instead of waiting to be asked yourself.
Practice entering a conversation. (Even if it doesn't always work.)
Think about what you would say in certain situations.
Don't be lazy about speaking up, say something.
Don't merely answer a question *Ja* or *Nein.* Support your answer, or give background information, or tell a story.

CONCRETELY:
Decide on a course of action for the next day: I will speak up in class at least five times, for example. Then check to see if you have accomplished this.
Consider who you would like to know better tomorrow, and plan appropriately.

AND FURTHERMORE:
Only when you are interested in others are you interesting to them.

7 GERMAN WITH GERMANS
TRAINING FOR THE COMPETENT:

THE WAY IT IS (FOR SOME):
Once you are an advanced speaker of a foreign language, it is difficult past a certain point to tell when you are making progress, though you are aware that you are far from perfect. Perhaps you really have stagnated. Some people stop trying too soon to make progress with a language.

WHAT TO DO?
Even if you are well-advanced in the language, you occasionally should concentrate on furthering your German—through intensive courses or other forms of concentrated language training.

HOW?
Decide which linguistic issues are still problematic for you, despite your advanced status. Then decide on a limited but intensive form of learning.

WE RECOMMEND:
Ask German friends to honestly evaluate your language skills, or a teacher for a professional "German-diagnosis" (see tip 26). Find a tandem partner to engage in challenging conversation with (see tip 1).
Ask yourself if there is, in your city or at your university, an intensive course or training course for advanced students.
If you are able to afford it, hire a professional intensive trainer. Institutions that offer German as a foreign language can be of help in your city, *Volkshochschule* (or VHS, institutions for continuing education), or the university.
Study the course offerings of the various institutions that offer advanced German courses (the Goethe Institute is one). There also are special certificates for advanced students ("*Kleines deutsches Sprachdiplom*," for example).

CONCRETELY:
Linguistic areas that are particularly suited for special training:
- pronunciation and intonation
- rhetoric and extemporaneous speech
- technical terminology and professional jargon
- styles of written expression
- German as a literary language

AND FURTHERMORE:
The point is not so much that you must speak German like a native, but that you not prematurely end the process of acquiring German. You will be motivated more effectively by short, intensive learning experiences than by continuous exertion. It is the mark of a strong personality and of respect for the foreign culture when someone who is competent is willing to become a student again.

8 GERMAN WITH GERMANS
GERMAN IN THE EAR

THE WAY IT IS (NO DOUBT ABOUT IT):
Today almost everyone owns a cassette recorder or walkman, but most people listen only to music. German textbook publishers offer extensive programs on cassette, but they are often expensive. Many German language teachers find that it is too complicated to provide their students with German texts on cassette. And so in the classroom there is too much "German on paper," and not enough "German in the ear."

WHAT TO DO?
Organize a "German in the ear" program yourself. Put your cassette recorder or walkman to professional use: Find your own German speakers.

HOW?
Each day, decide which texts are important to learn. These might be texts from an exercise book, texts you want to repeat or practice speaking, texts you need to know for a test, or which you simply enjoy (see tips 32, 35, 36, and 37). Among your German friends there are probably a few whose voices you particularly like; ask them if they will read the texts into the cassette recorder for you (see tips 1, 4, 6, 9, 10).

WE RECOMMEND:
We're not talking about perfection here; a voice that has traces of a dialect is not a problem and may even prove to be positive. The important thing is for you to like the voice, like to listen to it. Ask several of your acquaintances: different voices, both male and female, are better than only one voice, which you might soon tire of.

CONCRETELY:
Once you make a collection of tapes in this way, you will need to create a proper table of contents, so that you may quickly locate texts you need. You could have someone read the entire contents of your German textbook onto cassette. This is a particularly good way to practice listening comprehension, repetition of texts (for language tests), memorization of texts, and pronunciation and intonation (through simultaneous recitation). It is also a good way to practice specialized texts (important short, technical material, for instance), and last but not least, to prepare for a report or talk in German (see tip 40).

AND FURTHERMORE:
With this method you are actually organizing your own language lab, and establishing concrete, professional contacts with Germans, and making new and important contacts.
This method is particularly effective for all those who are anxious about speaking German, especially with Germans.

9 GERMAN WITH GERMANS
AN INVITATION TO GERMANS

THE WAY IT IS (SOMEWHAT OFTEN):

The preconception is that Germans are reserved people who live behind closed doors and have no time for others, and that it is not easy to make personal contact with them. This is true in part, and because some Germans are like this, and many foreigners believe they are, it is sometimes hard to establish contacts. For many foreigners this diminishes the opportunity to speak with Germans in the everyday course of their lives.

WHAT TO DO?

Don't wait for a German to issue an invitation, issue one yourself. Don't wait for Germans to open their doors, open your own. Be a host/ess in your host country.

HOW?

Observe how social contacts are organized in your immediate surroundings. Determine your place in this, and play an active role. Issue an invitation to a new friend, a neighbor, an acquaintance, and the rest will follow. You will see that a positive experience will result.

CONCRETELY:

Ask a neighbor to tea.
Ask someone to go to the movies or the theater with you.
Ask who would like to go to an interesting lecture, a rock concert, disco, swimming pool, jogging, to the sauna.
Celebrate your birthday with people you know.
Offer to show off your cooking skills.
Every day brings some opportunity, particularly on the weekend.

AND BY THE WAY:

Consider the fact that this same method is employed in high diplomatic circles: When a diplomat is on a state visit to a foreign country, at some point she invites the host to dinner at his or her own country's embassy. This shows respect both for the host and for the host's country, and is good for the cultural climate.

10 GERMAN WITH GERMANS
GET OUT OF YOUR ROOM!

THE WAY IT IS (MUCH TOO OFTEN):
The feeling that one is not truly at home in Germany, among Germans, often causes foreigners to retreat to the four protective walls of their own rooms or living quarters. It is good to be able to concentrate at one's desk or to leisurely read a book in bed. But it is not good to stay at home because you feel depressed or timid, or ill at ease. Sometimes foreigners do not even notice that Germans are celebrating their town festival that weekend, say, or that the Christmas fair has opened.

WHAT TO DO?
Do everything that brings you in contact with Germans, and is fun and gives you an opportunity to speak German and feel good.

HOW?
Don't stay in your room, go out and do something! (See tips 5, 6, 9, 11, and 42.) Overcome your inertia! Use the opportunities open to you.

WE RECOMMEND CONCRETELY:
Go to the movies often and take friends with you (instead of watching TV in your room or on your floor).
Stop by a pub afterwards for a beer and a talk.
There are discos in town, and people who would be happy to go with you.
Why not attend a theater performance or a concert now and then?
Have you – in the company of friends – been to the museums in your town or in towns nearby?
And have you made a small excursion into the outlying areas of your town? Go shopping in a town nearby, or borrow or rent bicycles and take a trip to the countryside. There are weekend places to visit where you can go sightseeing.
Every town has a calendar of events.
Read the local paper now and then. You will be surprised how much there is to do.

AND FURTHERMORE:
Get to know your German environs so that you may show a guest what is special about your town and your university, the beauty of your environment, or so that you know which pub to go to in the evening.

11 GERMAN WITH THE GERMANS
SHOW YOUR OWN CULTURE

THE WAY IT IS (WITH GERMANS):
Germans like to travel all over the world and are interested in foreign languages and cultures, but in Germany they often make their guests feel like foreigners.

WHAT TO DO?
Become an ambassador in German for your own country, your own culture and language. Present yourself as a professional interpreter of your land and culture. In contemplating what is essential to your own culture and your own cultural identity, you cease to be a foreigner in Germany, with Germans, and become someone who is accomplished and sought out.

HOW?
Organize occasions at which Germans will listen to you (see tips 1, 9, and 43). Seek out your own areas of expertise: as a speaker at lectures, seminars, slide shows, as a narrator, a writer, a co-worker or freelance journalist.

WE RECOMMEND:
Research which public event are held in your town or at your university, at which you might present something on your own country. And then make concrete suggestions.

CONCRETELY:
Speak with someone at the local school of continuing education; with institutions where your native language is taught as a foreign language.
Is there somewhere you might be able to teach your own language?
There are teachers in the schools who need up-to-date information on your country for their classroom instruction.
There are municipal, religious, student, and neighborhood activities to which you could contribute.
Express your opinions in a letter to the editor of the local newspaper.
There are political organizations that would welcome your proposals and like to work with you.
Perhaps there is a club or association that has as its goal the interaction between your country and Germany.
Clubs for senior citizens are always looking for interesting material.
Organize a festival with your fellow citizens where you share with others your culture and texts and music, at which you demonstrate your way of life, and celebrate it with your German friends.

AND FURTHERMORE:
Consider the fact that you are learning German among Germans as only half of the story. The other half is that Germans can and want to learn something from you.

12 WORDS
WORD-SCRAPS

THE WAY IT IS (MOSTLY):

If you're learning German you want, at some point, to be able to express yourself in German (almost) as well as you do in your native language. That, however, will take some time, and you will often feel frustrated when you don't know the right words and expressions. It is necessary to learn new words, but you may think, as many do: I'm not a schoolchild who has to practice my vocabulary every day. So the days pass, and you forget even the words you learned only the day before.

WHAT TO DO?

Make a game of learning new words and expressions by writing them on hundreds and hundreds of scraps of paper. This method has amazing advantages: It's fun, it's a way of taking many small steps, it makes good use of unproductive time, you learn through activity (rather than through passive reading), and you learn in a way that challenges your memory.

HOW?

1. Add this up: one sheet of paper folded in half becomes two sheets, and folded three or four times becomes 8 or 16 pieces. One hundred sheets will produce 800 to 1,600 scraps of paper.
2. Write all words that are new or unfamiliar to you on these scraps of paper: in class, when reading or doing your homework, when studying. On the reverse side, write whichever is more helpful to you: a) the translation of the word, b) a German synonym you already know, c) a (short) sentence using the word accurately. Method a is the simplest; but you might alternate the three methods.
3. Use the scraps to learn (or make a game of) according to mood and desire – at home, on the bus or a plane. Do this every day, with new or older scraps of paper.

WE RECOMMEND - CONCRETELY:

Deal out the pieces of paper as you would a game of cards and then collect those with words or expressions you already know. Don't throw them away, but save them to test yourself a second time. Those pieces left on the table are the difficult ones; these are the words you must practice often and repeatedly, until you are totally familiar with them.

Take a pile of these scraps (held together with rubber bands) with you when you go out, so that you may practice them. Take along blank pieces of paper and write down new words.

Limit yourself: 20 new words or expressions a day are plenty. That is 600 new words a month, or 7,200 a year: a powerful vocabulary.

AND FURTHERMORE:

If you make a game of learning with these scraps of paper, others will want to know what you are doing and some will want to imitate you.

This is also a good way to practice technical terminology (see tip 19).

13 WORDS
EXCURSIONS INTO A DICTIONARY

THE WAY IT IS (UNFORTUNATELY):

Many students of German possess only a small bilingual dictionary. Such dictionaries are necessary and useful (as long as they aren't too small), but they are inadequate if you wish to learn German well. If you purchase a larger, better dictionary you may not know exactly how to use it. But dictionaries are exciting, interesting, and useful tools.

WHAT TO DO?

Begin making excursions into the unknown realm of dictionaries. You will have interesting new experiences and a new way of learning German, full of adventure and knowledge. When used to translate words or to find a synonym or an explanation, a lexicon or dictionary becomes something more than a tool.

Dictionaries may also be used for systematic, entertaining learning.

HOW?

There are various types of dictionaries. In addition to small bilingual dictionaries, which can be stuck in a pocket and used daily, there are three types of monolingual German dictionaries:
1. dictionaries used to define and explicate words
2. synonym dictionaries
3. specialized or style dictionaries

These dictionaries are not designed to be carried around with you, but for use at your desk. There are larger (multi-volume) and smaller varieties. You should remember that the thinner the dictionary, the more sparse (and inadequate) the information. Consult your teacher for advice.

WE RECOMMEND:

There are various ways to play the dictionary game: a triangular excursion, for example. Begin with an expression and look up in a synonym dictionary which synonyms there are, writing down the more interesting ones. Then look up new words in an explanatory dictionary (which also supplies correct spelling and pronunciation, so you won't need a spelling dictionary). Then look in a style dictionary to place words in their correct context. It is amazing where you will end up.

You might also work your way systematically through a dictionary of meanings and write down those words (on pieces of paper, see tip 12) which appear important to you.

CONCRETELY:

Ask others how they work with their dictionaries. As with any other reference works, it takes some time to learn to use them quickly and effectively. But the rewards are great.

14 WORDS
DON'T TOUCH THAT DICTIONARY!

THE WAY IT IS (MUCH TOO OFTEN):
Many students, in reading a German text, read it word for word, and when they come across a word they don't know, they automatically reach for their bilingual dictionary. A minute or two passes until a (correct?) translation can be found; then it is back to laborious reading until encountering the next obstacle.

It is difficult to make progress in this way. Reading becomes a tedious activity, and one's understanding of the text is muddled or inaccurate. Reading is no fun this way, and will not help you make progress.

WHAT TO DO?
Don't touch that pocket dictionary when you read! Try rapid reading and marking your texts as described in the sections below (see tips 33 and 34). You won't need your pocket dictionary in most cases.

WE RECOMMEND:
Ask those sitting next to you in class for help. And the teacher.

Above all, read the text as a whole, not as individual words. Many of the words you don't know or immediately recognize will become clear in context, or prove unimportant; or you suddenly will recall the meaning.

(Only if you are alone and the unknown word or expression is truly pivotal, may you then use your dictionary, otherwise not.)

CONCRETELY:
You needn't leave your pocket dictionary at home, but don't use it when reading newspapers, in class, on the train.

You can break yourself of the habit of using the dictionary too often, just as you can break the habit of smoking or of eating too many sweets.

AND FURTHERMORE:
There are other ways of working with dictionaries that are much better and more educational (see tip 13). If you are reading a text, then read it. If you are listening to a lecture, then listen. You should not interrupt the important and challenging activities of reading and listening with leafing through a dictionary.

15 WORDS
WORD-GROUPS

THE WAY IT IS (MUCH TOO OFTEN):

Many people who study German learn words individually, one at a time. But words do not exist as isolated units in the dictionary; they are related to, or compatible with other words. They form "word-groups," and that is how they should be learned.

WHAT TO DO?

When learning a word, pay attention to the word-group and not just the single word.

HOW?

Look at the other words that form the word group and clarify the relationships between the words.

CONCRETELY:

With verbs: What is the noun form of this verb? With noun forms: What verb does this noun come from? (*unterscheiben/Unterschrift*)

With nouns: What verbs go with which nouns? (*Schloß oder Kirche: besichtigen/restaurieren/renovieren…*)

Many words have antonyms or negative forms (*erlauben/verbieten; erledigt/unerledigt; Arbeit/Freizeit oder Muße*).

Many words have groups of alternative choices (*Regen/Schnee/Sturm/Gewitter*).

Verbs/nouns have adjective forms (*Terror/terrorisieren/terroristisch*).

Many "German" words have relevant "foreign" equivalents and vice-versa (*Herstellung/Produktion*, see tip 18).

WE RECOMMEND:

Use this method in connection with the word-scraps method (tip 12) and the dictionary game (tip 13). You needn't always write down the words. You can also use this method as a mental exercise: When you find an interesting word, imagine other words that would form a word-group together with it.

16 WORDS
STICK-ON MEMOS

THE WAY IT IS (FOR MOST PEOPLE):
The human memory is one of nature's wonders. But often it doesn't function quite as we would wish; we forget too rapidly what we have just learned. Though we have practiced the new words of a text, we suddenly confuse them or they become vague, and that is aggravating when preparing for a test or an examination.

WHAT TO DO?
You might strengthen your short-term memory by writing what you need to learn on bits of paper, and sticking them to the wall next to your desk, or on any surface you look at often.

HOW?
There are useful pads ("post-its") that have an adhesive strip on the reverse side of each sheet. On these, write words or phrases in large block letters, then stick the pieces of paper wherever they will be effective.

CONCRETELY:
Consider the many small areas at home where it would be suitable to post such memos. Any desk area offers room for 20 or 30 pieces of paper; and then there's the kitchen, bathroom, hallway, mirror...

WE RECOMMEND:
Remove a piece of paper once you are sure of that word or phrase. Don't throw it away, but add it to your scraps pile (see tip 12). Once you have used that method to secure the word in your memory, then you may throw it away.
Of course, you shouldn't post too many pieces of paper at one time or the whole thing will become too involved and therefore less effective.

AND FURTHERMORE:
You might also use this method to learn short grammar rules, complete sentences, or short texts you wish to memorize (see tips 21, 27, 29, 35, and 36).

17 WORDS
"SNAPPED-UP" IDIOMS

THE WAY IT IS (IN A THOUSAND CASES):
If you're studying German in Germany, you have countless opportunities day in and day out to hear how Germans speak. (If you're not learning German in Germany, these opportunities seldom present themselves.) You will repeatedly hear idiomatic expressions that sound good, are formulated precisely, express the "truth," and "hit the nail on the head."

WHAT TO DO?
You must act quickly to "snap up" these words, expressions, idioms, metaphors, and formulations before you forget them. If you delay only a few minutes, it is already too late.

HOW?
Always carry with you a small notebook, or scraps of paper (see tip 12), or post-it pad (tip 16), and something to write with. You must be able to get to them quickly and easily in order to immediately snap up these morsels of the German language.

WE RECOMMEND:
The notebook or pieces of paper must be small in size and ready-to-hand; and the writing must go quickly. The whole process should not disturb the conversation or communication in progress.

CONCRETELY:
Small notebooks have the advantage of not falling apart; you can then copy them onto scraps (see tip 12) at home. This is a good way to practice the word or phrase.
Or you might wish to use a paper scrap to write the idiom down on, and then add it to your pile at home. The advantage of post-its is that you can post the piece of paper immediately where you can see it for a while (see tip 16).

AND FURTHERMORE:
This type of learning is particularly effective because you have heard the expression or phrase in a concrete situation, and can then place it in the exact context in which you yourself experienced it.

18 WORDS
"FOREIGN" WORDS ARE NOT SO FOREIGN

THE WAY IT IS (IN TODAY'S WORLD):
We live in an international culture. English increasingly is becoming the "lingua franca" in the spheres of science and international communication (in air travel, for example, and computer terminology). The international science community communicates in English; one may speak English in (almost) all countries and situations. A large part of the English vocabulary, however, has already been absorbed into other languages, especially into the "European" languages. These words are primarily of Latin or Greek roots, and they build the largest, and—in science and the public sphere—the most important, international vocabulary. In German, these words are called *Fremdwörter*, or foreign words, out of both fear and respect. Many of these words, however, belong to the standard German vocabulary of modern communication.

WHAT TO DO?
This vocabulary is easily learned, because many words of your own native language exist in a similar form in German. Even if there are minor problems, you can quickly add 1,000 or 2,000 words to your vocabulary.

WE RECOMMEND:
Buy a medium-sized dictionary of foreign words and expressions and draw up a relevant list of words for yourself.
The dictionary should not be too extensive; it needn't be a reference work for technical terms. It should contain all *Fremdwörter* that are have become a part of authentic, contemporary usage in German. Each week, work your way systematically through one or two letters of the alphabet, covering the entire book in two or three months.
On scraps of paper (see tip 12), write down those words which appear to be most important to you.

CONCRETELY:
Write down words belonging to a word family on one scrap of paper, for example: *organisieren/Organisation/Organisator/organisatorisch/(un)-organisiert...*
Often, these words are written differently ("music" in English, *Musik* in German), and pronounced differently. Clarify variations in spelling, pronunciation and stress (for example: *psychology* in English, *Psychologie* in German).
But pay attention to differences in meaning, which can be major (and which are called "faux amis" or "false friends," examples being: *"preservative"* in English, *Präservativ* in German; *"infantil"* in Spanish, *"infantil"* in German). There might also be what are called "connotative" differences in meaning (which means that in German a word may "sound" different than in the original language: *"capire"* in Italian, *kapieren* in German, for example).

19 WORDS
MY TERMINOLOGY DICTIONARY

THE WAY IT IS (WITHOUT A DOUBT):
If you are working or studying in Germany, you will experience difficulties in your field which your German colleagues don't have, for you must meet your professional requirements in a foreign language—German. Often, success in one's field will be impeded by the effort one must expend in mastering the language.

WHAT TO DO?
You can better your situation by organizing your study of the language wisely and consistently. Create your own way of learning the terminology you need for your work.

HOW?
There are technical dictionaries for every professional sphere. You will need these in your training, at your desk, and on the job. These are difficult learning tools, because they offer too much information. You can, however, organize your own professional glossary, much in the way you created your word-scraps (see tip 12).

CONCRETELY:
Paper scraps work better than vocabulary notebooks. Always carry a batch of paper scraps with you to lectures, classes and seminars, or while reading books or newspapers, so that you may write down important technical terminology. On the reverse side of the paper you might record short definitions or translations (or citations).

WE RECOMMEND:
Make a game of learning what is on these technical vocabulary scraps. You could post them at home (see tip 21), or carry them around with you to prepare for tests; you might exchange them with your colleagues who are learning the same material.

AND FURTHERMORE:
You could also include your professional colleagues in this learning method (in preparing for tests, for example).

20 GRAMMAR
PRACTICING NONSENSE

THE WAY IT IS (QUITE OFTEN):
Many people who are learning German are afraid of or reject anything having to do with grammar. There may be something to this, for:
1. In German, small words and endings conceal many difficulties, and make learning, and particularly speaking, difficult. It will take some time before you will be able to speak without making mistakes.
2. Grammar books and many examples and texts used to teach grammar are deadly dull, dry, and pedantic.

Both of the above can prove to be discouraging to your mood and determination when learning German.

WHAT TO DO?
Turn learning grammar into something fun, challenging, pleasant. Invent nonsense versions of important linguistic structures—inverted sentences, or song lyrics that have meaning, but a comic effect. (You can also ask your teacher to create or provide you with such examples or short texts, which you can then memorize.)

This method has the advantage of letting you concentrate your memory not so much on the grammatical problem as on the humorous content. The problem of learning grammar then resolves itself.

HOW?
With imagination, perhaps together with a partner. The best examples are often those one invents oneself, because they will be your favorites.

Pay special attention to your everyday conversations. Life often is the author of the best texts.

Take examples from newspapers and magazines.

Do you know the authors, magazines, or cartoons where German humor and nonsense verse can be found?

FOR EXAMPLE:
Pronunciation problems: *Raucher brauchen wir hier nicht.*
Writing s/ss/ß: *Nasse Füße machen Spaß, weißt du das?*
Verb forms: *Der Mensch denkt, und Gott lenkt.* Past tense: *Der Mensch dachte, und Gott lachte.*
Becoming acquainted with subjunctive II: *Wo kämen wir hin/wenn alle sagten/ wo kämen wir hin/und niemand ginge/um einmal zu schauen/wohin man käme/wenn man ginge.*

WE RECOMMEND:
Use your grammar book, reformulate the rules in your own style and according to your imagination. Don't worry – texts are not sacred. Exchange your ideas with others who are doing the same thing.

21 GRAMMAR
HOUSE ALTAR

THE WAY IT IS (FOR MANY):

Perhaps you have in your room or apartment a corner reserved for pictures or objects you particularly value: photos, pictures, souvenirs, sayings...a little "house altar," a "sacred" corner of sorts.

WHAT TO DO?

Set up a similar house altar for your work with the German language. You may have more than one: over your desk, around the mirror, on the inside wall of the closet, in the bathroom...

HOW?

Use pictures, charts, sentences you wish to learn, captions, newspaper articles, scraps of vocabulary, corrected mistakes.... Anything that helps you to learn and make progress should be pinned or stuck to a special corner.

WE RECOMMEND:

– using capital or block letters so that you may read them from a distance,
– situating your house altar where it is clearly visible, and easy to read from or make changes in (from your desk, for example),
– look at it once or twice daily; change or exchange something on it daily.

CONCRETELY (FOR EXAMPLE):

Check whether, or how, your memory deals with your house altar. When you have learned something well, remove it.

Apply the pleasure principle: This activity should be fun for you, enjoyable.

If you wish, you may add an aesthetic dimension to your altar by using drawings, decorative writing and embellishments, with the help of a computer perhaps.

Collect the papers you have put on the altar, in a file, for example.

22 GRAMMAR
MY FAVORITE MISTAKES

THE WAY IT IS (FOR ALMOST EVERYONE):
Perhaps you are familiar with the Bible saying about seeing the "speck" in your brother's eye, but not the "log" in your own. That is to say, you hear and "see" how many mistakes others make when they speak or write German, but prefer not to see or perceive your own. If you make a mistake and are corrected, you apologize. You feel awkward or embarrassed, because you are not yet at home in the German language. But feeling ashamed or apologetic is an unpleasant sensation, and unproductive as well.

WHAT TO DO?
Learn to recognize and to "love" your own mistakes. Deal with them productively.

HOW?
Arrange with a partner to write down or document your mistakes, and to correct and discuss them mutually (see tip 24). Your partner might be someone who is also learning German and has the same difficulties, or your tandem partner (see tip 1). Your partner should be someone you trust and can work with well.

Try on your own to create a productive relationship with your mistakes. Make of them something tangible, visible: Create your own catalogue of mistakes (see tip 12); collect your most interesting mistakes from corrected homework, texts, tests, and record them in a special "mistake-notebook," or on "mistake-scraps," etc. Turn them into something positive. Post the best examples on your house altar. There are many amusing learning games to be played with your own mistakes.

WE RECOMMEND:
Discuss this method with your teacher; with others who are also learning German; with your tandem partner.

Create with a partner who is also learning German a "mistake-trade" game, (similar to trading stamps or beer coasters). Compare your mistake-scraps, discuss them, try to analyze your mistakes, to explain them. Think about how to deal with and resolve them.

CONCRETELY:
This method functions similarly to the "word scraps" method (see tip 12): work with easy to organize scraps (color, for example), writing in large, clear letters; plot your progress by removing the mistakes you have mastered – but don't throw them away. They can be used later to test your command of them.

23 GRAMMAR
MISTAKE IMMUNIZATION

THE WAY IT IS (FOR MANY):
Everyone knows that to learn a foreign language one must work at it, and that mistakes are to be overcome only through constant practice. Most people, however, find practice arduous, and soon tire of it. They practice too little, have too little fun at it, lose their enthusiasm.

You can change that. Practice should be like a game, should be fun and funny.

WHAT TO DO?
Just like the "love your mistakes" method (tip 22), you should not reject your mistakes, but cultivate them, become conscious of them through a kind of theater.

This method is suited only to those mistakes that have a connection to the linguistic and cultural peculiarities of your own native language: endings, word order, sentence construction, typical pronunciation, body language. Mistakes made in using idioms also belong here.

Don't worry, you won't reinforce your mistakes with this method, but rather slowly learn to immunize yourself against the mistakes you automatically make. It's true! (Just as in medicine: Immunization doesn't make you sick.)

HOW?
Treat your mistakes as a monologue, exaggerate them, act them out, declaim them. Try them out in front of the mirror as you're going about your everyday routine: when brushing your teeth, bathing, combing your hair, etc. Take advantage of your creative moods. Make a ritual of declaiming your mistakes while walking around your room; give a little performance of them when you have guests; play "mistake theater"; relate them to others or have others relate their mistakes to you, elaborating on painful or funny misunderstandings caused by mistakes.

You may combine this method with tips 20 and 22.

WE DON'T RECOMMEND:
Using this method to make fun of others or to deride them.

CONCRETELY:
Start with a small repertoire of mistakes and see which sorts of games work for you.

A good beginning is to use difficulties in pronunciation: If you are an Italian, for instance, try speaking a short text "as Italian as possible" (in front of the mirror). Closely observe yourself in the process; exaggerate, use mime and gestures as aids...Then expand your repertoire with whomever you're playacting with.

24 GRAMMAR
RECORDING YOUR MISTAKES

THE WAY IT IS (FOR ALMOST EVERYONE):
Anyone learning German is going to make mistakes. If you ask a partner to correct your mistakes, the conversation will be constantly interrupted, and constant interruption is annoying and unproductive. And yet, you wish to have your mistakes corrected.

WHAT TO DO?
Not every conversation is suited to the correction of mistakes, but you and your partner can agree that s/he will keep a record of them.

HOW?
Your partner notes (or writes down) which of your mistakes are most conspicuous and which disturb him/her the most. Some mistakes are more marked or perturbing than others. Once several mistakes have been recorded in this manner, agree that your partner will describe to you his or her observations and reactions, and go into detail about them with you.

WE RECOMMEND:
Organize your mistakes on appropriate mistake-cards, the size of large postcards, for example, and give them to your partner to observe. If you have foreign friends who, like you, have problems with German, you can play the mistake-recording game with them.

CONCRETELY:
Combine this game with tip 22. Include in your own mistake-record all mistakes your partner has observed in you, and which the two of you have discussed as important and noteworthy.

AND FURTHERMORE:
This game is particularly suited to tandem partnerships (see tip 1): Each records the mistakes of the other.
Be careful, however: As with any game, it is important to set limits; too little, and you learn nothing; too much, and it becomes one-sided and leads to frustration.

25 GRAMMAR
CORRECT ME - I'LL SHOW YOU HOW

THE WAY IT IS (FOR MANY):

Foreigners who speak German well notice that others no longer correct them. Germans they are talking to don't want to be always interrupting the conversation (for whoever makes a correction interrupts the conversation). And correcting mistakes no longer seems necessary because what is being said has been understood. Foreigners themselves don't encourage correction if they are always apologizing for their mistakes. However: If one's mistakes are not corrected, one won't know which mistakes are being made.

WHAT TO DO?

Speak with the people you are most often together with about the way in which they might correct your mistakes. Agree on a method of correction which can take place without interrupting communication.

HOW?

Demonstrate to your partners how they should handle your mistakes. The initiative must come from you. You must tell them how to do it and work with them to accomplish this in conversation.

CONCRETELY:

You should be sensitive to situations such as:

When is it truly necessary to correct a false or unclear expression (word or formulation), so that the correct expression will be understood?

Which mistakes can be corrected without interrupting the flow of conversation? How is this done? (Discuss this.)

Which mistakes cannot be corrected without interruption?

It makes sense in some situations to merely note mistakes and discuss them later, in the context of conversation in German.

There are conversations the content of which is so important that the correction of mistakes is beside the point.

WE RECOMMEND:

1. There are certain mistakes (involving endings, *der/die/das*, or cases) which can scarcely be corrected without interrupting the conversation. In this case, your partner should note the types of mistakes being made, and discuss them with you later (see also tip 24).
2. There are certain important words or expressions which should be corrected immediately using as few words as possible, and in a helpful, low-key way.
3. Mistakes concerning sentence structure and word order can be called attention to using discreet gestures or hand signals (without words); this allows the speaker to correct him/herself without interrupting the conversation or losing the train of thought.
4. Mistakes can be discussed after the conversation has ended, but only if the contact and mood between partners is good.

26 GRAMMAR
GERMAN DIAGNOSIS

THE WAY IT IS (AS A RULE):
When you first begin to learn German, your day-to-day progress is clear; you know exactly how much you have learned. But if you are an advanced student it is harder to perceive your own progress, and this often leads to a false self-evaluation. Many believe they are "worse" than they really are; many believe they are "better." You need to know as accurately as possible "how good" you are.

WHAT TO DO?
Have a professional German diagnosis drawn up for you by an expert (just as you would go to a doctor to clarify a medical condition). Ask a teacher of German to objectively evaluate the state of your German knowledge.

HOW?
Tests and examinations during instruction serve a similar function, but there one is under pressure to perform. What is meant here is a voluntary and thorough diagnosis. Most German teachers know how to give one. You must, however, request one, and, like the teacher, you must make time for one.

CONCRETELY:
Prepare for yourself and your teacher precise questions on the following skills:
1. pronunciation and intonation
2. verbal expression
   a) morphology/syntax
   b) choice of vocabulary
   c) style and use of idioms
3. written expression (see 2 above)
4. verbal/cultural behavior (that is, how "German" do I behave when speaking, in conversation and situations with Germans?)

WE RECOMMEND:
Consider beforehand your own skills: How "good" do you think you are? Compare your self-analysis with that of your evaluator. Speak with your evaluator about his/her judgement; discuss appropriate methods to strengthen your weaknesses. Ask if, after a certain period of time has passed (several months, for example), s/he would be willing to give you a new diagnosis.

27 GRAMMAR
MY GRAMMAR ON CARDS

THE WAY IT IS (AS A RULE):
You have bought a German grammar book; it includes much important and relevant information. There is much to learn from it, but it is not intensive enough, for you cannot learn sufficiently by looking at a grammar book now and then.

WHAT TO DO?
Write your own grammar book. Learn by copying important points of grammar onto cards. Learn by writing down the material and organizing it for your own purposes. (This is sometimes referred to as "mind mapping.")

HOW?
Choose a card size that is practical, a 4" x 6" index card, for example, which holds neither too much nor too little information. A heavier paper stock is best.

Label each card clearly: "adjective endings," for instance, and copy the material you wish to learn onto it. It is best to use only the front of the cards, so that you may post them on the wall (see tip 21).

Eventually include all grammatical points that are most important to you.

WE RECOMMEND:
Use visual elements (colors, dots, boxes, outlining, underscoring). Your cards will be more effective the simpler they are to read and to scan at a glance. Write in a clear script. Test whether you get more from writing the cards by hand than with a typewriter or computer.

CONCRETELY:
What topics are suited to using learning cards? Actually, almost all of them:
- verb forms (including auxiliary and modal verbs)
- the importance of the modal verbs
- active/passive voice
- forming the perfect tenses
- attributes with present and past participles
- declination of adjectives
- declination of pronouns, articles, and nouns
- verbs with vowel changes ("strong/irregular" verbs)
- sentence structure and construction
- use of the conjunctive

AND FURTHERMORE:
As you write your cards it will become clear what you do and do not yet understand, and what your particular learning problems are.

28 GRAMMAR
SENTENCE DECODING

THE WAY IT IS (ESPECIALLY IN GERMAN):
German sentences can be frightfully long, particularly in scientific and legal texts, and in magazines and newspapers, but also in certain literary texts. In addition, in many sentences the verb, or an important verbal component, is positioned at the end. This sometimes makes it difficult to understand the structure of a long sentence on the first reading, which also makes it difficult to understand the content.

WHAT TO DO?
It is easier, of course, to read authors who write in a simpler German and use shorter sentences (see tips 32 and 37), but if this is not the case you must decode the sentence structure.

HOW?
You should not read a text word by word (see tips 33 and 34), rather, you should "scan" it. That is, you should go from the beginning of the sentence to the verb, and from there directly to the end of the sentence, where other parts of the verb might stand (*Satzklammer*). Then ask yourself: Who is doing what? What is occurring? Who or what else plays a role in the "story," in the "game" of this sentence? Then all other information will follow: when/where/why, etc.

WE RECOMMEND:
You might wish to accentuate this reconstructive, decoding work with a pencil or a marker, for sentences are often several lines in length. Practice this method until your reading of German texts becomes more intuitive. The important thing is first to decide how intensely you wish to carry it through. It counters tips 33 and 34 to a certain degree, but this is not a basic contradiction: decoding can go very fast. When it is important to comprehend a long text quickly, use this method only with those truly difficult, lengthy, and complex sentences.

AND FURTHERMORE:
In using this method you will be reviewing all of German grammar, for you will be reconstructing the grammatical/semantic structure of texts.

29 GRAMMAR
PHRASE PRACTICE

THE WAY IT IS (APPARENTLY):
Certain peculiarities of German grammar are hard to accept: You might learn the rules of grammar in a few minutes, but it takes months, sometimes years, before errors cease. And that is frustrating.

WHAT TO DO?
Practice grammar using phrases you repeat automatically, so that similar structures will also be automatically correct when speaking and writing German.

HOW?
1. Locate grammatical points and clarify the rules belonging to them.
2. Devise two or three concise examples (phrases) that are easy to remember.
3. Memorize these phrases by saying them aloud or writing them down repeatedly, until they come to you automatically.

CONCRETELY:
Here is a short catalogue of structures suitable to this method:
1. article + adjective + noun (variations of adjectival endings) (e.g. *ein kleines Meerschweinchen/einen alten Hut*)
2. the dative case following prepositions (e.g. *mit einem kleinen Unterschied*)
3. choice of the dative or accusative case (e.g. *Der Kaugummi klebt unter dem Stuhl/Ich klebe den Kaugummi unter den Stuhl.*)
4. placement of verb at the end of a sentence, following "daß." (e.g. *Ich weiß, daß ich nichts weiß.*)
5. verb as second element of the sentence and noun as third element, if the sentence begins with time or place (e.g. *Heute nacht war ich nicht im Bett/Zu Hause habe ich ein Meerschweinchen.*)

WE RECOMMEND:
Devise your own examples. (Combine this method with tips 8, 16, 21, and 28.) It doesn't matter how intelligent, comical, or funny they are: You must like them in order to repeat them automatically, much as a parrot learns to "speak."

AND FURTHERMORE:
When adults learn a foreign language, they need to vary their methods: some for the head, to serve understanding, and some they can mimic, repeat, work with automatically. Even an intelligent person can play parrot now and then.

30 GRAMMAR
DEFINE WHAT YOU WANT TO LEARN

THE WAY IT IS (OBVIOUSLY):

There are excellent textbooks and grammars, but many people who learn German make slow progress despite them. This is often because they don't know how to learn, or how to learn from books.

WHAT TO DO?

You must make the text and grammar books you have bought your own. Each day you must decide what and how much you truly wish to learn.

HOW?

Decide with each new chapter of your books, with each German class, what it is you really want to learn.

This is much like tip 28, and also tips 16, 21, 22, and 35.

CONCRETELY:

1. When you read a text decide which 20 words you want to learn and copy them down on pieces of paper (see tip 12).
2. When you find long lists of elements in your grammar book (irregular verbs; verbs with prepositions; simple and complex prepositions; conjunctions; modal particles, etc.), decide which and how many of them you want to learn, and over what period of time.
3. Proceed in the same way when you are working with long lists of words, idioms, or technical expressions.

WE RECOMMEND:

Again: Decide what you want to learn, and why.

Speak with others who are learning German and with your teacher about this method, and ask their advice. Speak with others in your German class about the method you choose.

31 GRAMMAR
WORKING WITH WORKBOOKS

THE WAY IT IS (QUITE OFTEN):
Sometimes one can look at a book and see that it has not been used often. How do your books look? Perhaps after a long time they still look relatively new. Try something different: You will get more from your books by writing in them.

WHAT TO DO?
If your book has a broad margin, use it to write down anything important. But don't mark the reading samples or fill in the exercises; you may then make use of them a second or third time.
If your book has exercises, write the correct answers in the margin, or even better in a notebook in which you do all of your homework. Then you can repeat the exercises in the workbook at a later date—without being able to see the answers immediately.

WE RECOMMEND:
If you write legibly in the margins of your book, you can cover the margin with a sheet of paper when you wish to repeat the exercises. Then if you have trouble with the answers you can quickly look under the sheet.

AND FURTHERMORE:
Include your marginal notes and your own answers to the exercises in your recapitulative learning. You will learn it more effectively.

32 TEXTS
LEARN BY MEMORIZING

THE WAY IT IS (FOR MANY):

Many people believe that memorization is dull, something for children. And since adults are no longer children, they no longer learn through memorization.

Some even believe that adults are not able to learn through memorization.

WHAT TO DO?

This, however, is incorrect. Memorization is a qualified intellectual activity, for adults as well. In memorizing a text one makes it one's own. And that goes for the language of the text too: Memorization is an important and acknowledged method of appropriating new language. You can learn German through memorization.

So memorize something; learn through frequent memorization.

WHAT TO DO?

Choose texts suited to memorization: poems, song lyrics, literary satires, texts you have written yourself, short literary texts...
Important criteria are:
You must like the text, the more the better.
It should not be too long (10 to 20 lines will suffice; one-half or three-quarters of a page, preferably shorter).
You must be able to memorize it well. The text must "sit" well.

WE RECOMMEND:

Locate books in which such texts are to be found (for example: Brecht's: *Kalendergeschichten*; texts by Kafka, Hesse's *Lektüre für Minuten*, short prose by Peter Bichsel and Max Frisch's *Tagebücher*; as well as many children's books. There are collections of these texts available.) Ask your teacher for titles, or ask for suggestions in a bookstore or library.

CONCRETELY:

Copy texts you wish to memorize into a journal, or for your "altar" (see tip 21), or a "wall paper" (see tip 35). Use your cassette recorder (see tip 8). Memorize a new text each week.
Recite or speak the text in front of the mirror or before a few listeners or an audience.
You can make a communicative game of it by reciting literature together with others.

AND FURTHERMORE:

You will discover that memorization is fun.
You will find that people enjoy hearing texts recited from memory. If you know the lyrics of songs, join in the singing.

33 TEXTS
RAPID-READING

THE WAY IT IS (NOT INFREQUENTLY):

Many people read too little. If you cannot read a book in German then you have not learned the language.

Many people do not read the newspaper. If you do not read the paper regularly, you cannot get to know Germany.

But texts are often guite long, and you may quickly lose the fortitude to read and comprehend an entire text.

Some people read too slowly, word-for-word; all of the words and phrases you are unfamiliar with make this type of reading laborious. You soon tire, and then stop altogether.

There is also a cultural problem. Many people have too much respect for the text. A text on paper is not something sacred. It is not individual words but the sense of the whole text that should be understood. Texts should be cracked open like nuts. And as quickly as you are able.

WHAT TO DO?

Practice rapid-reading. Daily. With every text you read.

Rapid-reading should be employed at the first encounter with a text. (Just as you form a spontaneous and immediate impression of someone on first encounter.) Rapid-reading is a cultural technique. You should attain the same speed when reading a text in a foreign language as you do in your native language.

HOW?

First, see how long the text is: 20 lines, 3 pages, half of a newspaper page, 25 book pages...

Then make a prognosis of how long it will take you to read it. The first reading should tell you what the text is about, its message, its chief information.

Then read rapidly through the text, trying to maintain a constant speed.

But remember: rapid-reading is not a sport to be engaged in with a stopwatch. You want to understand the text, and reading should be a pleasure.

CONCRETELY:

Get some idea of the content from the text's title or caption. If you are reading a magazine text, photos will help. Choose a reading speed somewhere between scanning and reading for detail.

Don't use a dictionary! (See tip 14.) Instead, try to understand words you don't know from the context. (Not all unfamiliar words are important in the comprehension of a text.)

Ask yourself if you have understood (roughly? precisely?) what was said in the text, in the passage.

34. TEXTS: READING WITH A MARKER

THE WAY IT IS (SOMETIMES):
Many students of German have too much respect for the paper their texts are printed on. But they throw newspapers away after they read them. And write or draw in their exercise books. Printed literature is seldom materially valuable; its value lies in its content. And that only if it is dislodged from the paper and stored in human consciousness.

WHAT TO DO?
Curtail your respect for the paper the text is printed on. Use pencils, ballpoint pens or felt-tip markers to mark texts with lines and color.

HOW?
Use markers on your text to mark words, expressions, sentences, or passages that are important.
You can order the content of a text with markers.
Marked texts can then be studied at a glance; those places that are important are immediately visible.

WE RECOMMEND:
Purchase markers in various colors (there are markers now available that have fewer chemicals). Light colors such as yellow and orange are easier to read through than blue, green or pink. Too much marking, however, makes a text hard to read.

AND FURTHERMORE:
You will note (in preparing for a test, for instance), how quickly you will remember the information in a text when you scan the marked passages.

35 TEXTS
COLLECTIBLES

THE WAY IT IS (IF YOU OPEN YOUR EYES AND EARS):

Many people, as children, collected things that interested them, and continue to do so as adults. Perhaps it's no longer beer coasters, but books, photos, texts, pictures, letters...

The collected items are material objects, but they also embody experiences, feelings, and knowledge. You keep something because it was important to you emotionally or as an experience.

WHAT TO DO?

If you are learning German, begin to collect interesting and important items from the German language.

HOW?

Anything that spontaneously arouses your interest is of value and should be added to your collection. The sole criterion is that it must appear interesting to you spontaneously.

CONCRETELY:

There are many things to collect: short texts (see tip 36); long but important texts; photos that invoke commentary; caricatures and cartoons, jokes and pointed opinions, "words of the week" and bonmots; catchy advertising slogans; your own journal entries; points of discussion or argument you have "snapped-up"...

There are no limits, but the item must appear to be truly important, for this linguistic find then becomes a part of you.

And remember: not only positive, but also negative, unsettling, or strange items belong in your collection. These then become "barbed bits" of knowledge (see tip 43).

WE RECOMMEND:

Clarify how you wish to collect things. A file binder is easier to organize than a standing file box; you will learn more if you post the items (as a constantly changing exhibition) than if you keep them in a shoe box. There are clear sleeves that can be held in a loose-leaf binder; and thick paper to glue things to, as in a photo album...

AND FURTHERMORE:

You could show your collection to others; explain and clarify why you find something important; make gifts of individual items, as collages, for example.

36 TEXTS
MY MOST FAVORITE TEXTS

THE WAY IT IS (ABSOLUTELY):
Everyone has books and texts in his or her native language that are particular favorites, that one has spent time with, made a part of oneself. One lives in such texts.

But you do not yet feel so at home in a foreign language, though you are moving in that direction. Each German text that you especially like is an important sign that you are making the foreign language of German a part of you. Each new favorite text is a success you should be congratulated upon.

WHAT TO DO?
Discover your favorite texts and collect them in your own archive.

HOW?
You may consciously seek such texts during instruction, in the literary section of a bookstore, while reading newspapers and magazines, in the public or university library, in conversation with your teacher or German friends.

WE RECOMMEND:
Figure out a system for saving your favorite texts. (You could copy them and put them or paste them in a notebook.)

You could exhibit them where you can see them (see tips 21 and 35).

You could enlarge them on a good copier and add a graphic design.

AND FURTHERMORE:
Perhaps your friends would enjoy your favorite texts. You are letting your friends get to know you better through your favorites.

37 TEXTS
BEDSIDE READING

THE WAY IT IS (OFTEN ENOUGH):
Many students read only those texts that appear in their workbooks or textbooks. That is not enough. There is more to reading than that: Reading is a journey of discovery, an adventure.

WHAT TO DO?
"Reading" can mean reading the newspaper, for example. But above all it means reading literature; light literature and belles-lettres. It also means reading daily.

HOW?
Reading functions when it is enjoyable. So you must find texts that you like, that aren't too complicated (that is, you don't need a dictionary to read them), and that aren't too long, so that you will finish them.

Also, you can always put a book or a newspaper in your pocket, to read when you have time: while waiting for a train, on breaks, during your occasional spare time.

And above all, before falling asleep.

WE RECOMMEND:
Let your teacher, or someone who knows German literature and the book market, recommend something suited to you.

Inquire about titles in a bookstore or library. Speak with other foreigners about suitable titles in German.

Appropriate are: short stories; novellas (which aren't as long as novels); contemporary light fiction; children's books (which aren't written in complicated language and often have large print. There are wonderful, funny, intelligent, and exciting children's books available); mysteries and suspense novels; and certain authors whose style is relatively simple (your teacher will be able to name a few.)

Certain newspapers and magazines have a simpler style than others, for example: *Stern,* as opposed to *der Spiegel* or *die Zeit*, which is to say nothing against them (see tips 33 and 34).

CONCRETELY:
Find a favorite reading place in your town, residential area or university where you can read undisturbed and comfortably. There are cafes everywhere where you can read (see tip 46).

AND FURTHERMORE:
As you read, you will get an idea how far along you are with your German; if you are carried along by the suspense in a mystery, for example, your difficulties are behind you. When a literary text begins to appear "wonderful" or "important" to you, you have found a new language in German. Then it is time to also begin writing in German.

38 TEXTS
LEARNING WITH COMICS

THE WAY IT IS (PERHAPS):
German often appears difficult to those who are learning it, and learning is sometimes boring. Comics can help with this—a fact to which most foreigners will attest. They are familiar with comics (for both children and adults) from their own culture, and with caricature and satire as well. When they are good, comics and cartoons are entertaining and funny.

WHAT TO DO?
Learn German with comics and cartoons that have been written in or translated into German.

HOW?
There are bookstores everywhere that carry comics.
Many English and French comics have been successfully translated into German. Less well known is the fact that there are wonderful German comics, cartoons and caricaturists.

WE RECOMMEND:
Ask your German friends to name their favorite strips, titles, authors. Do you know the work of Seyfried, Waechter, Gernhardt, Buchegger, Loriot, Clodwig Poth, Marie Marcks?

CONCRETELY:
Comics and cartoons are living examples of the spoken language. Check it out.

AND FURTHERMORE:
You can make a game of translating comics into German yourself. For example, you could make a copy of the comics, screen out up the words in the bubbles and make up German texts for the stories. It is fun to then compare your version with the original, or with the printed translation.

39 TEXTS
TAKING MORE PROFESSIONAL NOTES

THE WAY IT IS (FOR MOST PEOPLE):
In German class, in your training courses and seminars, in lectures, it is always the same: Information, useful formulas, and important notes are written on the board. Much of it you wish to write down, and perhaps you do, but your notes look disorganized— slapdash handwriting, everything mixed up together, little pieces of paper, big pieces of paper. It's a mess which later is of little use to you.

WHAT TO DO?
Create your own blank forms on which to take notes in class, in your seminars and lectures.

HOW?
Each person has his or her own way of writing. Some people have small handwriting, others, quite large. Some require lined paper, others need large amounts of blank space; some prefer their paper in a small format, others can write only on single sheets, and still others in bound notebooks or books. Decide what is best for you.

WE RECOMMEND:
Create your own forms with a felt tip pen and a ruler, or on the computer, and make copies of them. In this way you will be able to take notes more professionally.

CONCRETELY:
Important are:
1. a top line on which you can write a heading (a key word for the contents)
2. a wide margin – at least 1/4 of the sheet – to hold your own comments, for ordering the content, important tips, a later reworking of the text, and for corrections.
3. a space in an upper corner for the date and page number.

This leaves roughly two-thirds of the sheet for you to take notes on; but your notes will be easy to manage and have a well-organized design, with comments on the what, when, where, why, and purpose of the subject.

AND FURTHERMORE:
You will quickly notice the usefulness of this method if:
you are taking more notes than usual;
if you are recording what is essential and important;
if you look over your better organized notes later and can read them more easily.
Ask others who are studying or learning with you how they take notes; show them how you do.

40 TEXTS
MORE PROFESSIONAL TEXTS

THE WAY IT IS (PERHAPS):

When you write in German, your language and style will not be as accurate as someone whose native language is German. Texts often serve an official function: important letters, texts written for publication, papers to be presented in class, in your studies at the university or in your profession...
If you must hold a lecture or write an official letter, you are at a disadvantage in German. You may not know what to do in such a situation.

WHAT TO DO?

Edit your text carefully before you let it out of your hands. Prepare yourself extensively before giving an oral report or a lecture in German. Work professionally with German in your training, your studies, your profession.

HOW?

Something you should not do is to pay a German to edit or alter your text or make it more "German." Rather, find a German you trust, together with whom you can edit your text. An intensive cooperative effort between you and your German partner will produce a fitting German formulation for what it is you wish to say. This will take time, and possibly money, but it is an effective way to learn German.

WE RECOMMEND:

Combine this method with the tandem method (tip 1). Ask your colleagues in class or at work if they have the time or desire to invest in this type of intensive cooperative effort. The institutions for German as a foreign language can help you find a suitable partner. You could also ask your university lecturers for assistance in finding a partner.

CONCRETELY:

If you must give a paper or a lecture, find a German who will read your carefully edited text onto a cassette tape; then you can practice speaking the text. (Your audience will thank you for it; see tip 8).

AND FURTHERMORE:

This is a fair and correct method; even German scientists and speakers in the economic and political spheres make use of it when they must give or write a paper in a foreign language.

41 TEXTS
READING ALOUD, DECLAMATION

THE WAY IT IS (VERY OFTEN):

When you read a textbook or technical material or fiction at home, you usually do so silently. People read aloud much too seldom, and there is too little recitation and declamation.

WHAT TO DO?

Only the spoken word can truly be called speech. Reading aloud at home, without an audience, is an intensive type of reading. You are practicing not only reading with your eyes, but pronunciation and intonation as well, and in addition, you are hearing yourself read.

HOW?

For a few minutes each day, make an exercise in learning and concentration by reading aloud a text you are already familiar with.

WE RECOMMEND:

Practice aloud using gestures and declaiming, as if before a large audience which, is listening to you closely and which you wish to captivate. Literary texts serve this purpose better than non-literary. When reading aloud, stand or walk back and forth, or use a lectern, if you have one.

Use a cassette recorder occasionally, to be able to listen to your voice.

And remember, when reading aloud raise your eyes, look up from the paper into the room (or into the mirror, at your "public.") Don't continually look down, but ahead now and then; it opens up speech.

CONCRETELY:

When reading aloud, you are automatically practicing pronunciation, grammar, vocabulary, and idioms. You will notice how often you pause or stumble, and how fluid your German is, or isn't.

You should practice reading aloud to the point that you can get through sentences in one breath, without stopping or correction.

AND FURTHERMORE:

Consider whether long pauses while reading aloud in German have something to do with fear. Learn to treat German without fear. Free yourself up in your newly-acquired German language.

42 GERMAN IN GERMANY
"CONQUER" GERMANY

THE WAY IT IS (FOR SOME, UNFORTUNATELY):

"Learn German in Germany" sounds good, but many people don't use the opportunity. They go to classes and do their exercises, but their German surroundings remain foreign to them. They associate with their own compatriots, or hide among them.
Is this due to fear? If so, something should be done about it. Too complacent? Not interested? That would be too bad.

WHAT TO DO?

If you have the chance to learn German in Germany, you should "conquer" Germany every day, continually. To do this you will need courage and enthusiasm. In exchange, you will enjoy success, and have fun, and new experiences.

HOW?

"Conquering" does not entail an arrogant, overbearing onslaught. As a foreigner, you have rights and opportunities and you should use them. Each day, plan an adventure, whether large or small; something other than what is scheduled or planned for the classroom. Speak with friends about your experiences; in doing so you will receive new impetus.

CONCRETELY:

Here are a few suggestions:
– Go shopping at the weekly market and talk to the people there.
– Find a cafe or pub in your town or neighborhood you like to visit in the afternoon or evening, someplace you can engage in conversation.
– Go to bookstores or the library to "browse" (see tip 46).
– There are libraries where you can hear recordings of German texts.
– Are you familiar with the museums in your town or neighborhood?
– Weekends and holidays are good times to plan something with your girlfriend or boyfriend.
– If you are active in sports at home, why not join a sports club in Germany?
– Become aware of the cultural, political and social "scene" in your town. Would you like to join a choir, an orchestra, interest group, a congregation?
– Are you familiar with the educational facilities (*Volkshochschule*) in your town, the cultural program?
– Read the local paper to find out what's going on, what's interesting, and how you can participate. And so forth...

43 GERMAN IN GERMANY
DIARY OF FOREIGNNESS

THE WAY IT IS (MORE OR LESS):

If you are living and learning German in Germany, this does not mean that you have immediately found a new homeland. Often, you may feel that Germany and the Germans are strange to you. You yourself feel you are a foreigner, which can be painful or frustrating, even be perceived as a crisis. But this situation can prove productive: as a new and different experience, an alternative to your own way of life up to now. But also as critical distance, in order to see Germany and the Germans more clearly.

WHAT TO DO?

Become as conscious as you can of what is strange to you about Germany and the Germans: the language, the country, the people, their way of life, their mentality. Record your observations and your feelings of strangeness. Be a meticulous and sensitive observer. Write a "diary of foreignness."

HOW?

Everything that occurs to you is meaningful enough to be recorded: what you find odd, what you like or find insulting, what appears exemplary or repugnant to you, what amuses or stimulates you.

WE RECOMMEND:

You need only a good notebook or diary for your observations, one in which you enjoy writing. It should not be of disposable design, but one to be carried with you for a long time.

CONCRETELY:

You might record your observations on:
– food, drink, habitat, buying, celebrating
– TV (news, commercials, entertainment)
– your image of the city in which you live; the people there
– how Germans act in an official capacity, their way of presenting themselves
– Germans' orderliness, disorderliness
– fashion, Germans' aesthetic sense or lack thereof
– kinds of fear, kinds of courage

What you write will surely be an interesting and meaningful report on your encounter with Germans, and on your time in Germany.

AND FURTHERMORE:

You will see how your competence and self-confidence grow in dealing with Germans. It is possible that you yourself will change in the process. Your feeling of foreignness will change as well.

44 GERMAN IN GERMANY
MY GERMAN DIARY

THE WAY IT IS (OR COULD BE):

Perhaps you have heard it said: "When you dream in German for the first time, then you know German, then it has become your new language." And it is true that whoever dreams in German has found an unconscious access to the German language.

What you record in your diary are daydreams, as well, of course, as your experiences, reactions, occurrences, thoughts. But because a diary is for you alone to read, your entries address your individual identity, both actual and ideal. You are speaking to yourself and to the person you wish to be.

WHAT TO DO?

Write in German – keep a German diary. It will importantly document that German is your new language.

HOW?

Anyone who has ever kept a diary knows what it is about: writing in a diary is similar to meditation, prayer, reading, to writing a letter to a good friend or someone who is important to you (see tip 43).

WE RECOMMEND:

Create for yourself a space for quiet, a time for quiet and concentration; have your notebook ready and then simply begin.

Write at regular intervals, twice a week, for example, or every other day.

CONCRETELY:

Simply start writing. It isn't a matter of producing "good" texts, it's not about work; leave your dictionary and grammar book out of it if they interrupt your writing. Your entries do not need to be polished, you can use catchwords (see tip 43). Choose a notebook or book you enjoy using, one that is employed only for this purpose (not for notes or shopping lists, etc.).

AND FURTHERMORE:

Your diary entries in the new language of German are documents of your life, your work, your personality. You can change the texts or correct them. You can give your friends texts you think are good or important. Perhaps you could publish part of it, use it to write a letter to the editor. If there is an extemporaneous writing class offered, join it.

45 GERMAN IN GERMANY
SEPARATING FROM YOUR COMPATRIOTS

THE WAY IT IS (UNDERSTANDABLY):

There are several advantages to learning German in Germany: for one, you are constantly surrounded by the German language. But there is a disadvantage as well, and that is that you are far from home. This can lead to homesickness and create the tendency to seek out frequent and intense contact with your fellow countrymen, whom you can communicate with without difficulty. It is understandable to want to maintain and cultivate your own cultural identity. But it can diminish (or even hinder) your success in learning German and getting to know Germany. If this becomes a habit, you don't give yourself a chance to experience the German language and culture. You end up hiding in your group of compatriots, in the culture of your homeland, and as a result Germany and the German language remain strange to you.

WHAT TO DO?

Spend part of every day away from your fellow citizens. Avoid them a little, without being impolite or losing contact with them.

HOW?

Energetically pursue contacts with Germans (see tips 1-11). Ask yourself what kind of contact with your compatriots is truly important to you.

CONCRETELY:

At the end of each day, calculate how much German and how much of your native language you have spoken, with whom and why. What could you have done differently, better?
Think about which German contacts you can deepen.
Try speaking German with your own countrymen. It will probably seem artificial, but treat it as a game and it can be fun.

WE RECOMMEND:

Consider what it is you wish to achieve:
– completing specialized training in the German language, being able to read German literature
– learning German, perhaps as a foreign language, perhaps as a new language for yourself
– getting to know Germany as a new culture or as your own land.

46 GERMAN IN GERMANY
MY SECOND WORK SPACE

THE WAY IT IS (ALMOST EVERYWHERE):
Everyone who lives in Germany has a room or an apartment where s/he is "at home," where there is a desk, a work space, to learn German. It is from here that one goes back and forth to class, to work, to an institute or school or university.

WHAT TO DO?
You can do more. Find a second work space to study German. Your first work space is in your room; where is your second?

HOW?
Where you live there is surely someplace you can read and study undisturbed; where you can set up a second work space for yourself, where you can keep several books. It could also be the quiet corner of a cafe, or a peaceful meadow.

WE RECOMMEND:
A place where you can go for an hour or two each day to concentrate on your work and read, someplace close to books, someplace less isolated than your room or apartment. Someplace where there are other people who also are working, whom you can observe and talk to.

CONCRETELY:
The advantage to a second work space is that you can move around a little as you undertake to learn German; a change of place helps you endure minor frustrations and feelings of resignation. You needn't stay seated in any one place for too long; you have another choice of location in which to get a second wind.

AND FURTHERMORE:
You can test the effectiveness of this method yourself: The second work space is the right place to be if your creative juices begin to flow there, if new ideas occur to you, and you can concentrate on your reading and writing.

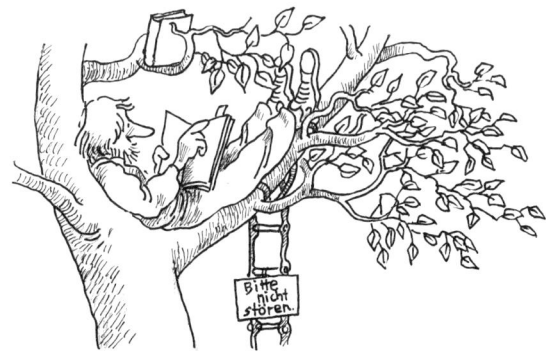

GERMAN IN GERMANY

47 MY DAILY NEWSPAPER

THE WAY IT IS (IN THE FOREIGN LAND OF GERMANY):

If you are living, studying and working in a foreign-language environment, you won't feel like you are "at home." You miss your daily newspaper, radio broadcasts in your own language, TV programs that you are familiar with. The German media are different than those at home. But if you don't read the German papers or watch German television, the German language and customs will always seem strange to you, and you will remain a "foreigner."

WHAT TO DO?

Familiarize yourself with the frequencies of public and private radio stations. Use German TV, and not only the on/off button; read television program listings. Our tip: *Tagesschau*, *heute, Tagesthemen* and *heute journal* report on everyday German life. Take a look at regional programming as well. And as for newspapers, read one for a few minutes every day, truly every day, even if it requires effort at the beginning.

HOW?

Every knows how to read a newspaper. But you have to be willing to do it: in a corner of the library, on the train or a city bus or in the subway, on a park bench, or before going to sleep. And at breakfast, of course.

WE RECOMMEND:

Read without a dictionary, simply proceed even if you don't understand every word; scan a text, look at the headlines (see tips 14, 33, and 34); read only what truly interests you; buy a newspaper daily or often (which is better than reading merely what you find lying around).

CONCRETELY:

STERN and *BILD* are easier to read than *DIE ZEIT* and *DER SPIEGEL* (each person will have to decide which magazine s/he finds more informative).

We won't suggest which supraregional newspaper would best inform you about Germany, the world, or your own country, but the following are the leading German daily and weekly newspapers: *Frankfurter Allgemeine Zeitung (FAZ), Frankfurter Rundschau (FR), Süddeutsche Zeitung (SZ), Die Tageszeitung (taz), Die Welt, DER SPIEGEL, DIE ZEIT*. Become a local in your own region; that is, read the local section of the paper.

You could also read a professional journal in your field.

AND FURTHERMORE:

You yourself will note when you are making progress. When the daily paper becomes easier to read, when you enjoy it and consider it essential reading, then you will feel more at home in Germany.

48 GERMAN IN GERMANY
BOOKS USEFUL IN LEARNING GERMAN

THE WAY IT IS (FOR MANY WHO WISH TO LEARN GERMAN):
Each person has some German books or other: a textbook for learning German as a foreign language, a grammar, one or two dictionaries. But there are other interesting titles with which you can learn German.

WHAT TO DO?
Find out which books will be helpful to you. Create your own small working library for German as a foreign language.

HOW
Go to a bookstore in your town and look at books on the subjects of German as a foreign language, German literature, and the study of the German language and linguistics.
Speak with your German teacher about books useful in learning German. Look at the brochures of leading publishers of books on German as a foreign language.

CONCRETELY:
– Would a second textbook on German be helpful to you? Is there a text written for your level of learning that would help you to progress?
– Do you have a good, comprehensive monolingual German dictionary?
– Do you have a good German book of synonyms?
– Do you have a good dictionary of foreign words?
– Do you have a good dictionary of style?
– Do you have a text to help you expand your vocabulary and use of idioms?
– Do you have a good, extensive German grammar to use as a reference work?
– Do you have a condensed grammar?
– Do you have a "contrastive" grammar for German/your language?
– Do you have a book that deals with mistakes in German typical of speakers of your native language?
– Do you have a good anthology of German literature, of contemporary German literature?
– Do you have a book on Germany and German culture that is easy to survey, a map of Germany, a good travel guide?
And so forth...
You could assemble, say, ten books of the above types on your shelves or desk.

AND FURTHERMORE:
Each year there are new and attractive books designed for learning German. Keep yourself informed of them.

49 GERMAN IN GERMANY
MASKED FOREIGNERS

THE WAY IT IS (FREQUENTLY):
If you are learning German in Germany, you may sometimes feel at a disadvantage when speaking German. No matter how good your German is, the Germans always speak it better, and are more at home in their surroundings. In many minor situations (and sometimes in a dramatic fashion) you are made to feel that you are a foreigner. And that can make you feel depressed or aggressive.

WHAT TO DO?
Now and then, create some distance between you and your German surroundings; create a certain feeling of superiority you can "mask" yourself in – as a foreigner. Play to the hilt the foreigner who understands practically nothing.

HOW?
This is a method to be used in situations of conflict. It can also simply be a game, not to be taken seriously. Either way, it puts you at a certain advantage. In presenting yourself as more helpless than you are, you become something other than a hapless foreigner. Rather than suffer inconsiderateness, arrogance, or displays of sympathy, you can wait for the moment to play your cards right.

WE RECOMMEND:
Play this rather spiteful game in small doses and consider it carefully beforehand: at times when you feel overwhelmed, or need some breathing space. It is possible that out of this will come a serious discussion on the conflicts and potential of intercultural coexistence.

CONCRETELY:
You can expand the game by carrying with you a hidden microphone and cassette recorder. You will discover that Germans have their good sides (a willingness to help and exert themselves) and their bad sides (inexperience in dealing with, or a superior attitude toward, foreigners, rudeness, sometimes even racism).

AND FURTHERMORE:
In particularly unpleasant situations, if someone is treating you rudely as a foreigner, you might also simply go on the offensive and address them aggressively in your own language; refuse to communicate with them in German. You are demonstrating that s/he can also be the "foreigner" in certain situations. You will find that you may get amazing results with this surprising reaction. Sometimes the other person will suddenly become much friendlier.

50 THE LAST TIP
CREATIVE REFLECTION ON LEARNING GERMAN

THE WAY IT IS (HOPEFULLY):

Each person is creative, has creative moments in which one sees oneself in a clear light, recognizing one's own strengths and weaknesses.

WHAT TO DO?

Use these creative moments to write down what you could do differently, or better. This is the time in which to make plans.

HOW?

Take a sheet of paper or your diary (see tip 44), and begin recording your own personal situation: How effectively, creatively, are you learning German? Keep what you write, and reread it later.

WE RECOMMEND—CONCRETELY:

Asking yourself concrete questions:
- Which personal or professional goals do you wish to attain with German?
- How good do you want to be, how good are you now?
- Where do your weaknesses lie? (See tips 22 ff.)
- How have you utilized your time up to now?
- Do you feel at home in your German surroundings?
- How freely do you deal with the German language, which difficulties do you have in using German?
- Which things are fun for you? Which are no fun at all?
- Which things are you totally unable to do?
- Is there something you particularly would not like to hear said?
- What are you afraid of?

It is good to speak with a friend or partner about your analysis of yourself. And then to draw practical consequences from this creative reflection.

AND FURTHERMORE:

You are on the right path if you are always clear with yourself about what you truly wish to attain with the German language.